Moses Hartz
GREAT-GREAT-GREAT UNCLE

by
Jonathan F. Stoltzfus

Moses Hartz
Great-Great-Great Uncle
by Jonathan Stoltzfus

Copyright © 2013

Library of Congress Number: 2013956795
International Standard Book Number: 978-1-60126-411-4

Printed 2013 by

Masthof Press
219 Mill Road
Morgantown, PA 19543-9516

TABLE OF CONTENTS

FORWARD

This essay on the pro and con of how the Amish people keep the shunning towards members who have been excommunicated is a search for deeper understanding of what the Bible teaches on shunning and how this is administrated in view of the Moses Hartz controversy in the Amish congregations of Lancaster County, Pennsylvania.

We have here an overview of two hundred years of church discipline showing how this discipline concerning the shunning of expelled members has had some variation of change through the years.

The roots of the Amish and the Mennonites go back to Menno Simons, a Catholic Priest who studied the scripture where he found, then accepted, salvation full and free through Jesus the Messiah, The evangelical people in the Netherlands at that time were the Waldensens whose leader had been Peter Waldo during the twelfth century, then spreading all over Europe with no connection to the Catholics: The Waldensens had come to a low ebb, and when Menno Simons came on the scene they accepted him as their leader in 1536. He mustered the true New Testament believers together from among the Waldensens who now became known as Mennonites, and expelled those from the fellowship who were living in sin. The Swiss Brethren became a part of this renewal during the reformation but it seems their culture clashed somewhat with ideas in the Netherlands as Jacob Ammon differed somewhat with them in 1693. A good insight in this can be found in "Letters of the Amish Division" by John D. Roth and Joe Springer, 2002.

In the seventeen nineties the revivals of John Wesley began sweeping across America. The Amish were right in the middle of these places of spiritual renewal, many of them becoming Methodists.

In 1820 many people in the Conestoga Valley met in the woods of Robert Jenkins close to Churchtown, today known as "Narvon Station," where John Summerfield, the Methodist preacher from England preached to over a thousand people night after night. In 1840 similar meetings were held at a pine grove east of Morgantown where large crowds came and camped for a week at a time under the preaching of Methodist preachers. Apparently the 1809 discipline where Amish Bishops agreed on much stricter church rules as a way to hold their members together, many of whom were joining other church denominations, but their stricter rules lasted only slightly more than a generation until a division occurred among them. It seems that in every Amish division shunning became one of their sore spots.

When there is dissatisfaction in a church among the adult members of a congregation, the young teen-agers are often the ones who absorb the most painful part of these interactions, especially if one has a tender heart and is already a sincere believer as to knowing who Jesus is.

According to Jonathan Stoltzfus who grew up in an Amish congregation where a church division is pending, or could we say coming to fruition just before 1966. Those who then pulled away in this division became known as New Order Amish. The part that Jonathan has difficulty accepting is that during that time setting he was expelled from the fellowship of the church because he missed the communion service twice and is now shunned by his people. He has made an extensive study of the Amish methods of housekeeping concerning what the Bible teaches about the Ban and shunning. This essay brings out some of the unsolved problems of the past that seem to be open ended yet today.

-Christian P. Stoltzfus

INTRODUCTION
PART I

This writer was a great great uncle at age 50, by virtue of being the ninth of ten children. His father was the youngest of seven children, making us "hinter nachkomme." Inasmuch as the writer has roots in the Conestoga Valley by birth, and is directly affected by the early events there, this becomes partly a biography and partly an autobiography.

Father and Mother were good parents, though they had their share of grief. Mother Katie was part of an easy-going family, called the Buck Dave family, living on present day Route 897 where once the Buckley Forge was located on the Pequea Creek where it crosses that route. Her Mother Katie (Fisher) was living near Gap, Pa., less than 6-months old, when President Lincoln's funeral train passed through Gap on the way to Philadelphia and New York and to Illinois. I was 14 when she died at our house.

In 1855 Mother's Great Grandfather Daniel Mast, a minister from the Conestoga Valley, near Morgantown, went to an ordination service in this lower Pequea area near Gap.

He invited 35-year old Moses Hartz to go with him. As Providence would have it, the lot fell on Moses, who then ministered there a few years before locating again permanently at Conestoga as a minister. At that time there were only five or six Amish church districts in Lancaster County. There is reason to believe that church districts worked back and forth, and because of distance, church services were held only by-weekly.

My father Gideon, who grew up very close to my mother's homeplace, tried to follow the example of Jesus, the Good Shepherd, according to God's Divine Order of Creation, I Cor. 11:3. Plain people of various persuasions do quite well in the practice of family shepherding, and showing respect for them, and with symbols of respect. Scripture teaches that fathers are the family and church family shepherds. But sadly a few do sometimes act as family sheep dogs. Perhaps many of us do sometimes.

I often think of something my father said a number of times, at home and perhaps in sermons. He said, "Leaving the church is like leaving your wife or husband, and leaving your wife or husband is like leaving the church." I don't recall that he meant a particular denomination, but to point out the seriousness of leaving the church and especially our faith in Jesus Christ. We all want our children to keep our beliefs and traditions, as our ancestors desired the same in their native countries. But some of them, because of persecution or other reasons left the traditions of their forefathers while remaining faithful to Jesus who died for them. What my father said made a lasting impression on me, and gave me a vision that actually comes from the Bible, of Christ and the Church, the body of believers. That relationship should draw us close to the One who died for us, and to glorify our Eternal Father in heaven. Our earthly relationships must give way to the heavenly, "For in the resurrection they neither marry nor are given in marriage, but are like the angels in heaven," Jesus said. Mathew 22:30.

INTRODUCTION
PART II

Many of my generation, siblings, cousins and friends have passed away. What does the future hold? Let us continue faithfully walking with the Lord, keeping His commandments, bearing the Gospel message of Christ the Passover Lamb. I write from my own experience, and partly from other sources as will be mentioned.

It is in the nature of being cut off from family, church family and homeland, to not have the normal channels to do research and to provide details when undertaking a project like this. And yet there is homework to be done. I know what it is like to be cut off, as we will see later on. Now I find myself living in the land of Goshen, Indiana, married to a Hoosier native, Marietta, daughter of Elam and Eliza Hochstetler. This family has long been good to me.

I have chosen to use a reverse time line, basically a 200 year period from the year 1966 back to the year 1766, when Nicholas Stoltzfus arrived in Philadelphia, Pa. We have been doing vegetable farming since 1971 in an area once largely inhabited by Dutch immigrants from the Netherlands. I have had conversations with people who remembered when their church here on our street changed from using their native language in their services, to using English. They had large acreages of celery and perhaps similar crops, farmed with horses at one time, letting them roam the neighborhood when not in use, so they said. Many of these people have passed away in these 40 years. We live on the former Marchand 8-acre celery farm. The house was built in 1906 and ten children were in the family, two of whom, Garret and Walter (Farmer) operated in partnership selling door to door, until 1970.

Soon after my conversion to Christ in 1955 I started using the "Our Daily Bread" devotional, which was begun in 1956 by a Dutchman, Dr. M. R. DeHaan in Michigan. He was first a house calling country doctor in Byron Center, MI, beginning in 1914, using horse and buggy. Incidentally, I once went to that area to pick cabbage plants for my own use in the fields, taking my nephews with me.

For a long while this devotional used the King James Version of the Bible, but now their Scripture texts are basically from the New King James Version. I appreciate that, since the KJV has long been respected and widely used, although the New International Version is the main version in our church.

While some Bible translators are much concerned about "inclusive language" for God the Father and for brothers and sisters in the Christian faith, the NKJV still freely uses pronouns for the Holy Trinity. A good example is Isaiah 53, a passage about Christ the Suffering Servant. Those pronouns are actually capitalized, to distinguish between the Holy Trinity and human beings. Also the word brethren is still used in referring to the brotherhood of believers. Is anything wrong with that? The recent teaching that "In Christ there is no male nor female," should not be taken literally, as is often taught in this present 40 to 50 year "sexual revolution," Many people have been mislead and even deceived by that and we can see it in the gay movement. This movement by its very nature is the complete antithesis (opposite) of the relationship of Christ and the church, His holy bride. That gay movement should be assigned the heading of antichrist, which the Bible speaks about. In this writing, the NKJV will be used as the main Scripture text.

INTRODUCTION
PART III

"But God forbid that I should boast, except in the cross of our Lord Jesus Christ, by whom the world has been crucified to me and I to the world." Philipians 6:14

West of Morgantown, Pa. on Route 23 a few miles, by Maxwells Hill, is an old little red school house. Nearby there was once a stone quarry and in the midst is where Christian P. Stoltzfus grew up. He now lives in the same area as where I live and he is married to a Mast, a Hoosier native.

I am very grateful for him and give credit to his writings, which he frequently shared with me, a while before he published the book, "Amish Church, School and Historical Events." He is twelve years older than me, but we have been acquainted since I was a young boy, seeing him with young people. Once it was at a church service at the home of my Uncle Aaron and Aunt Betsy Beiler. While waiting for lunch he did some acrobatic stunts on overhead pipes. We were at one time a part of the same youth group, but most of the time he was away doing mission work in Canada and in South

America. I enjoyed corresponding with him by mail. He goes by the name Chris, which rhymes with the word "this." The name Christian is a very noble name and is widely used among the Amish people. Another common short version is Christ, not pronounced as the name of our Savior, but pronounced to rhyme with the word "mist," and as the first syllable in Christian. Perhaps this is as it should be with the two shortened versions. The name Jesus is common in some cultures as a given first name for men.

Also I give credit to and thank J. Lemar and Lois Ann Mast of Masthof Bookstore at Morgantown who wrote, A History of the Conestoga Mennonite Church called, "As Long As Wood Grows And Water Flows." The Conestoga Creek begins in this area and extends the length of Lancaster County and flows into the Susquehanna River. The Conestoga Mennonite Church had its beginning just west of Morgantown soon after the 1877 Amish Mennonite division. At that time they became known as Church Amish, while those who stayed with the lone Amish minister Moses Hartz, became known as House Amish. This phrase above was coined by the local people from the town of Morgantown.

Also, a few miles south on what is now Route 10 is where I worked at a potato harvest for Jake Mast in 1960 and in 1961, the first year picking in pairs into baskets with my second cousin Mayme Stoltzfus, granddaughter of Dad's Uncle Benemal of this valley. I did not realize it until many years later that this potato farm was once the farm of the Moses Hartz family. In my early years I had heard the name and had heard of the "schtreng meidung," (strict shunning) but I really did not know the story. Some have said that the meidung always was that way. I think not quite. This story was not freely talked about where I grew up, only about ten miles southwest of there.

I am also indebted to "Mast Family History," by C.Z. Mast, who co-authored "Annals of Conestoga Valley," and to "Fisher Family History." My father had Mast as his middle name and I have Fisher as my middle name. Back in the sixteen hundreds the name Stoltzfus had been written "Steltzenfuss," which says in German "he who has stilts on his feet."

ANCIENT TIMES
CHAPTER 1

"For whoever desires to save his life will lose it,
and whoever loses his life for my sake will save it."
Luke 9:24

This is something that we all should learn. It is one of life's most important disciplines, sometimes learned easily, and sometimes learned the hard way. I believe that Moses Hartz learned it. I believe that Joseph the son of Jacob, learned it in Egypt. I am learning it while being in a lifelong shunning discipline and having been disinherited.

Our Lord Jesus knew about it when He gave Himself up on the cross to make atonement for sin, by the shedding of His own blood. This was done once, for all time and for all who would believe in Him. How precious He is!

The Prophet Isaiah prophesied, "He was taken from prison and from judgement. And who will declare His generation? For He was cut off from the land of the living; For the transgression of My people He was stricken." Isaiah 53:8.

How encouraging are the words of Isaiah. "Surely He has borne our griefs And carried our sorrows," Jesus was cut off from His own people the Jews, as the Prophet had said, after He had been given a natural, or supernatural, birth here on earth.

Joseph was cut off from his homeland, "stolen away from the land of the Hebrews," from the family that gave him birth and who nurtured him into his teenage years, only to be sold as a slave by his brothers, traded to Egyptians by his cousins, or second cousins, Ishmaelites from Midian. Both Ishmael and Midian were sons of Abraham. But the promise was established through Isaac. Genesis 17:21. But the Lord was with Joseph. Four times that is said in chapter 39. What an encouragement!

Later the ten older brothers came to Joseph in Egypt where he was put in charge of the grain harvest, and then to distribute it during the famine. He recognized them but they did not recognize him. Through an interpreter, they said they were honest men; although they had not told their father Jacob what really happened to Joseph. Jacob would surely have looked for his lost son. "Then they said to one another, 'We are truly guilty concerning our brother, for we saw the anguish of his soul when he pleaded with us, and we would not hear; therefore this distress has come upon us.'" Genesis 42:21. Imagine how Joseph must have felt when he heard this. God's time had not yet come to make himself known. He needed to hear more, which he did the next time they came, as he patiently waited on the Spirit of the Living God to lead him. While he was in prison, Pharaoh's chief butler, or cup bearer was released from prison according to a dream that he had. Joseph told him to, "remember me when it is well with you." But at the end of that chapter of Genesis 40, it says that, "the chief butler did not remember Joseph, but forgot him." Few people remember Moses Hartz but many people are persecuted for righteousness sake because of what was done to him. Unlike Joseph with whom things were made right, Moses was already almost 78 years old when he and his wife were banished permanently, and he lived another eighteen years without things being made right for them, and he died at age 96.

He was cut off from his father and mother by their deaths, becoming an orphan at age 4, in Berks County, Pa. But he and his wife were further cut off from the land of the living in their later years. But this was not so much by the discipline of the ban, for which they had made confessions and were restored. But by what took place after that, when without further going out of bounds, the ban was reinstated, never again to be lifted. It has been said that the ban has never been lifted in Lancaster County(as though it should be that way) for anyone after they joined another church. That is not true. Moses and his wife Magdalena did make confessions in the meeting house church where they had been received, when peace was made, and then the house Amish accepted this, the ban was then lifted, and they were restored. But only temporarily, as we will see in later chapters.

1966

CHAPTER 2

*"You therefore must endure hardship
as a good soldier of Jesus Christ."
II Timothy 2:3*

In the year of 1966 my wife gave birth to our first child, named Lonna, born 200 years and two days after Nicholas Stoltzfus arrived in Philadelphia. He immigrated from Zweibrucken, Pfaltz, Germany. He grew up in a Lutheran family, then married a girl of the Anabaptists and therefore was made to leave the land. We assume that he left the Lutheran church, to become a member of her church.

Also in 1966, Katie, 16 year old daughter of an older brother died (of a brain tumor). We went to her funeral from Colorado Springs, Colo. where I had served in alternative service [1W], at Memorial Community Hospital.

This was the year of a Amish church division which affected a large part of Lancaster County. For a number of years there was unrest and great concern about a number of innovations that were making their way into Amish farms and homes. As always, this raises concerns about family life and community, "Gemeinschaft," that is a word that was often heard in conversations and in sermons.

The issues involved basically six items: Grain combines, forage harvesters, barn cleaners, manure loaders, electric generators, and home freezers. We worked together in community with other members of the family and extended families or neighbors who were farming, to harvest wheat and oats, silage corn, and in tobacco harvest. The latter was mostly hand labor and went on into the winter to process it.

And now, fifty years later, Amish farms and businesses have many new inventions. This all makes the Hartz family at Morgantown seem so ancient. And still the "schtreng meidung" for those who were disciplined earlier for the same kinds of things, goes on and on.

For some time these new ideas had been in use in various places, but now it was becoming more widespread. I lived at home and served my father on our dairy farm until age 21 in 1961. That's when I became "of age" and was allowed to earn and keep my own wages. Even here, five years before the church division, I was hearing a lot about the unrest. I often overheard my father, a bishop, and others talking about it. The decree to make those six items unacceptable came in 1963 as a result of the annual county wide ministers meeting. I remember one previous occasion when that meeting was held at our place, when I helped to unhitch the horses from the buggies or carriages, and taking them to the barn and feeding them at noon, while Mother, with some help, fed the ministers.

Already in 1961 at least, as I was hearing these things, it became very unsettling to me to the point of not having a desire to participate in the fall council meeting and communion. I did not attend either one, and soon afterward I left home in very stressful circumstances, and spent the winter in Florida where I had a job and had my first date. So I missed communion that fall and also the next spring.

The 1966 division, with one minister in the district of my uncle, Bishop Buck Sam, and another minister not in agreement with the 1963 decree, resulted in the formation of the New Order Amish. Until the next communion service, those who joined the New Order Amish were not placed in the ban. One of my married brothers did join the new church about five years later, was put in the ban, where for us there is no end. My friend Chris joined the new church right away and was not put in the ban.

1955-1959
CHAPTER 3

"But what does it say? 'The word is near you, in your mouth and in your heart' (that is, the word of faith which we preach): that if you confess with your mouth the Lord Jesus and believe in your heart that God has raised Him from the dead, you will be saved. For with the heart one believes unto righteousness, and with the mouth confession is made unto salvation. For the Scripture says, 'Whoever believes in Him will not be put to shame.'" Romans 10:8-11.

What does it mean that Jesus was raised from the dead, but that He first died on the cross to make atonement for our sins. Oh what love He has shown us!

We understand that this Scripture shows what all must do in every generation in order to be saved. Among the Amish people where I was born, this usually takes place when young people become serious about making wedding vows, sometimes earlier and sometimes later. For me it was earlier, at age fourteen, one might say by accident. But really, one should say it was by Divine Providence.

At age fourteen a young Amish boy is not expected to get serious about spiritual things. If they do, then older ones sometimes don't quite know how to handle it. My family said it was the accident that changed me, and "Yonie was never the same since." As I learned about this false report of my accident over fifty years later and how it came to our children, it was grief, and it caused confusion in my present family about me as a person, and about my mental health, and about my Christian testimony. It is like saying, "He's not all there." God knows. "For God has not given us the spirit of fear, but of power and of love and of a sound mind." II Timothy 1:7.

The farm accident happened on June 23, 1955, the actual day, according to a get well card from my Aunt Betsy. As us three youngest brothers were preparing at noon to make hay, the horse Bobbie that I was hitching to a wagon, suddenly jerked sideways due to a sore shoulder. It knocked me over and my head landed hard on the driveway. My two older brothers then carried me unconscious to the house into a room where they treated me the best they could, where I stayed until my parents came home a few hours later. They and my two sisters were at a weekday church service at my oldest brother's place near Gap in a neighboring church district of Uncle Buck Sam for a visiting minister named Ira Nissly. I was there on June 23, 2005 when my brother was not well. Grandmother Katie, mentioned earlier, died earlier this year of 1955 in this same room at home with uncles, aunts and our family gathered around.

Our house calling doctor treated me for a couple of days before deciding to send me to Lancaster

General Hospital. Until then I remembered only that Mother woke me from time to time to give me medicine. At the hospital it was found that I had a fractured skull, a concussion, with internal bleeding.

It took surgery to remove the blood clots and a spinal procedure to relieve the pressure, and I soon felt better, but it took weeks of recovery and some chiropractic treatments.

During the recovery I received many get well cards that are still with me, and some gifts were given. One gift was a small book called, "Stories of the Gospel." These were Gospel stories that Jesus taught, including many parables. This really meant a lot to me, and really touched me and made me want to give my heart to Him and to confess Him as my Savior, the one who died for me and gave peace and joy in my heart, saving my soul from eternal condemnation. I don't know who did this kind deed for me to give me that book. God knows. I was so grateful. I don't know where the book is today.

At age sixteen young people are expected to begin "running around," and to fellowship with other young people in various activities. In our area some of those activities were not very well acceptable, leading some astray. For me, it was something that I dreaded. So I stayed home for three months until I had enough courage to contact my cousin's son, John. He belonged to what was called, the Group, perhaps three or four dozen young Amish youth of various ages. Their activities were more Christian oriented and were more encouraging to me. But our group was not well accepted among some people, as in my own family, where I had some opposition. Out of respect, I hesitate to say much on this. But now there are reports that Christian activities are more accepted and supported. I felt led to be baptized in the Amish church, which took place near my nineteenth birthday in 1959. I was not forced.

I grew up with a happy childhood, under Christian teaching at home and church. At Waterloo, a public school at Cains, we had good teachers, as well as Bible teachers who came weekly helping us with memory verses and Bible stories. I did not go beyond 8th grade, and not quite to age 14, because of an accident on the ball diamond at our White Horse School. But just before I went into IW service I started a high school correspondence course with American School in Chicago. As we returned from service in Colorado our car and trailer caught fire in an accident. I did not replace my textbooks after that.

We nearly lost our four month old daughter Lonna who was in the back seat. We barely had time to get unbuckled, as seconds after we got her out, the ruptured gas tank exploded and all was engulfed in flames. This happened in 1967, near Chicago, at Matteson, Ill. on the Lincoln Highway. It was close. "By the mercies of God we were not consumed." We also have a son Curtis, and a daughter Rosetta.

1909

CHAPTER 4

"However, when He, the Spirit of Truth has come, He will guide you into all truth; for He will not speak of His own authority, but whatever He hears He will speak; and He will tell you things to come." John 16:13.

1909 was the year that a new congregation began, which later became part of a new denomination. How did it come to be? As we will see in the following chapters, there was a growing dissatisfaction about the way that Moses and Magdalena Hartz had been treated in 1897 and how this affected other people who were making changes, and what it was doing to relationships; people on both sides of the isle with parents and their children, siblings, cousins, various relatives, friends and neighbors.

On September 29, 1909, a group of about 35 Amish families from various church districts met together out of concern for the ongoing situation where the age old practice of the meidung had recently become the "schtreng meidung," of shunning indefinitely those who left the church, which continued on and on and was becoming stronger, with no release. This group, with no ministers among them, wrote a petition and presented it to the bishops for consideration at the upcoming ministers meeting.

The petition as translated from German which Chris Stoltzfus included in his aforementioned book, is as follows: September 29, 1909

"Dear Ministers and Brethren;

First a greeting of love and peace from the brethren in the name of our Lord Jesus Christ, Amen.

We request a discipline after the old foundation according to the way that it has been taught to us in earlier times by the old bishops as to how we should keep the meidung? We are asking that you stay with us if we can stay together. If not we plan to draw away. We want to give you time until your next minister's Conference. We will come the next day for an answer, if we live. We hope and pray that you will accept us in peace, in the name of our Lord, Amen."

This was given to Bishop Henner (Henry Stoltzfus) and again Chris includes a copy of their response in German as it was given, and in English, dated October 12, 1909.

It begins:

"Greetings with love and peace toward all trustworthy brothers and sisters, by which this writing has come in our hand. We request your prayers and our wish is that all of us might stand in the truth until the day of our end through Jesus Christ, Amen.

There has been a writing handed to us. But just to think not one signature has been included therein. Yet Christ teaches nevertheless that he who abides in the truth comes to the light. Under ordinary circumstances, a person usually gives very little attention to letters which have no signatures included because a man has no idea what kind of a person you are dealing with. Therefore we will give an answer accordingly to all of whom it may concern.

In the writing there is a confession that you are requesting a discipline according to the way that the old bishops taught about the article of meiding. That is indeed a good confession but it was a detrimental idea that you did not make yourself known, as you want to be drawn together.

This is an awesome and sad saying. But if your confession is truthful we will then accept you in peace. Yes, our confession is likewise. We will see what the old bishops and ministers taught about those who are leaving, and the meiding, forty, sixty and to a hundred years back. We don't want anything except staying in that which we were taught, to be grounded in the truth in the apostles and prophets where Jesus is the chief cornerstone.

In the year 1861, the bishops of the holy church were, David Beiler, Christian King, Johannes Stoltzfus and Christian Umble. This David Beiler was then in his 75th year and they requested that he should write down what the rules of the old discipline were among them, which he did. Of the bann and the shunning he wrote that the unfaithful that leave the church and those who are fleshly minded will be expelled and put into the ban. But with true repentance they should again be taken in. After these guidelines have the old bishops also taught that the bann and shunning should not be lifted unless true repentance and remorse is shown for their sins.

In the year 1809, a hundred years ago, there was a ministers conference where part of the agenda was a decree that all who join another church shall be expelled and the meiding shall be kept towards them, according to God's Word and the apostles teaching, until they are again received in the church. But those who unknowingly overstep the meiding can be excused if they confess their fault before the congregation. Those who overstep deliberately must then be dealt with and expelled. According to the decree we confess the elders taught us from Christ and the apostles words. Jesus Christ taught us in Mathew 18:17 of those who do not hear the church, to keep them as sinners and publicans.

We don't find in the evangelical Word where we should keep a person otherwise. But when he repents, he shall again be taken in as a member. By this teaching we desire with God's help to stay and encourage and admonish all the brothers and sisters to willingly and honestly work together so that all of us may keep communion together with God's grace and honor. Amen.

Christian King
Henner Stoltzfus
Gideon K. Stoltzfus
Johannes Beiler
Benjamin Beiler
(The Bishops)

Chris Stoltzfus notes here that they "did not consider the fact that during earlier times when a church member would be expelled from the fellowship of the church, then join with another church, proving himself to be a worthy believer in the congregation, that a letter of recognition would then be given and the bann and the shunning would then be lifted." As in the 1966 division, those 35-40 families were then released without being expelled, and then formed their own congregation. It was first called the King Church, then the John A. Church, then merged with the Beachy Church, named after Minister Moses Beachey of Somerset County, Pa. What about the mention of a ministers conference 100 years earlier? What was this about? I wondered and wondered. We will see in a later chapter what it was about.

As for now, who were the five bishops? Two are unknown to this writer but I do know of the other three; Henner Stoltzfus was the son of "Millcreek John Stoltzfus," a prominent bishop in the 1800's. Benjamin Beiler was the son of Minister David Beiler Jr, and grandson of Bishop David Beiler, who was mentioned in the bishop's response. They will be considered in later chapters. What was this all about?

Gideon K. Stoltzfus was my grandfather, who died in 1934, the father of my father, Bishop Gideon M. Stoltzfus, who was the father of my brother Gideon K., at one time the bishop at Weavertown Church (1980-1996). This is the congregation mentioned above which began with those 35 families. What does all this mean?

Grandfather Gideon lived in the lower Pequea District, a half mile from the old Buckley Forge, the Daniel Buckley place, later to be the Buck Dave farm where Mother grew up. My parents were second cousins. Grandfather Gideon married Sarah Stoltzfus in 1877, who was from the Conestoga Valley. She would have grown up under the ministry of Moses Hartz, who was ordained in 1855, just three years before Sarah was born. She died young, only 2 ½ years after the events of 1909, in the year of the Titanic, one hundred years ago, in 1912. She died exactly ten years after her mother passed away. It seems she would have pleaded with her husband Gideon concerning Moses her minister at Conestoga and her people there, to have mercy. This area was an early home of the Dienner family in the U.S.

In the year of Brother Gideon's death (2004) while visiting with him and his wife Susie in Florida, a 3 day trip and for that reason only, and not being aware of a heart condition that he might have had, I also visited a first cousin, Gideon Stoltzfus, age 91. How many Gideons were there? Before I was born he had been a hired man for my young father. He said how my Dad had remembered going with his mother from close to Gap, to Morgantown (13-14 miles over the mountain) to visit his Grandmother Rachel in her last days. Dad was only about four and one half years old at that time.

1908
CHAPTER 5

"For I determined not to know anything among you
except Jesus Christ and Him crucified."
I Corinthians 2:2.

How many heartaches, headaches and conflicts could be
avoided if only we would hold to those words of wisdom! If
only we would keep foremost in our hearts those words of the
Apostle Paul, regarding Jesus who gave Himself up and died
for us.

1908 came before 1909. What was this year like? One of
the main persons in the 1897 events before this was Minister
David Beiler Jr. who died in early 1908. Then in the late summer of 1908 a meeting was called to deal with the meidung of
Moses Hartz and his wife. More and more people were being
put in the ban, many just for leaving the house Amish church,
making it hard to have good relationships with families and
friends. In their youth, my parents had many close friends
among them.

The unrest caused some people to join the Jehovahs Witnesses. My Great Uncle Jonathan, a brother to Grandfather Gideon, was ordained as an Amish minister in 1907, but then soon joined the Jehovahs Witnesses. I remember an occasion in my youth when my family was passing through the town of Intercourse one summer evening, when we met Jonathan's son Aaron who was a taxi driver. He was talking about someone to whom he had given instructions and said, "then he did not do what I told him to do." I bring this up as a way of connecting. Jonathan was born after his 4 year old brother Jonathan had died, with a brother Isaac born in between the two. Dad may have known him well.

During this time some people were using telephones, which was not quite acceptable, so there was shunning on this issue also. After counsel was taken for direction, three bishops from Ohio were called in to help. A young Amish minister named Stephen F. Stoltzfus, brother to John A., Grandmother Sarah's first cousins, wrote about all this, which Chris Stoltzfus included in his book. On September 15, 1908, these bishops met with 30 ministers of Lancaster County. As Stephen wrote, the results were:

"First: So long as the reprimanded Minister (Moses Hartz Sr.) will not keep the meidung towards his son and so long as others who now leave the congregation then join with the other church even if they are not in the bann, the meiding shall now follow. All members who at the present time change their membership to the Meeting House Congregation shall be shunned.

Second: Now if the reprimanded Minister (Moses Hartz Sr.) will keep the Meiding toward his son, then bring a letter of good report from his congregation to the ministers of the House Amish Congregation and the others who have gone over there who are also in the ban will bring a good report. Then the meiding shall be lifted from them.

Third: The telephones are very lightly looked upon, whereas the lay people have no convictions to get rid of them and cannot get themselves to put them away. Underwritten by us the following bishops and ministers: Jonathan Troyer, Jacob D. Beiler, Noah Beachey and all 30 ministers of Lancaster County, Pa."

This has the appearance that the life long "schtreng meidung" could not be discontinued as long as Moses Hartz Sr. is living. After all, how could they discontinue the "schtreng Meidung" on others as long as it is applied to Moses, which was not likely to happen, what with all the animosity at this time towards him? Moses lived another eight years after this. Magdalena died in 1901. The decree concerning them was supposed to be temporary, not carried out indefinitely. Not only was the above decree supposed to be temporary, those who were close to this situation as Chris heard it from his grandfather and from many of their elders in that generation, understood it to be specific that after the death of Moses Hartz it should then be lifted church-wide. Moses and Magdalena did their part by their confessions at the April 16, 1897 meeting, (to be explained in Chapter 7). But Moses lived on and on until he was almost a hundred. By then bitterness set in whereas the bishops left things as is without lifting the Bann as promised. How many times have I heard it said that I did not keep my baptismal promises? Oh my. Who were the bishops at the time of Moses' death in 1916? Perhaps some or all were the same as in 1909 who rejected the petition that was brought by the 35 families who were disturbed by the unresolved events of the previous year of 1908, which was brought on by the transgression against the Hartzes in 1897. Is'nt it peculiar that the ban would not be lifted again for them as long as he was living, and that steps to make this right would not be taken while David Beiler Jr. was still living? It seems that a confession from him, even on his deathbed, would have made many things right.

Actually, the first and second items speak of two different issues; in the first, "others who now leave the congregation," in the second, "and others who have gone over there."

In his aforementioned book Chris reports that one of the Ohio bishops at this 1908 meeting, later, on his deathbed, pleaded for someone to go back to Lancaster County and make things right. He was not at peace with what he had helped with in Pennsylvania. We don't know if anyone tried. Is it too late?

As the results of that September 15, 1908 conference was presented to the congregations, many were not in agreement, and some members stayed back from communion.

And to think of all those who were disciplined because of the telephone, and many of those never had the ban lifted, yet the lifelong "schtreng meidung" goes on and on over one hundred years later. And there is widespread use of telephones among the Amish, as though no one had ever been disciplined.

Where is the "Amish Forgiveness" we hear about in recent years at Nickel Mines? We have to think of the words of the Prophet Jeremiah in Lamentations 3:22-23, "Through the Lord's mercies we are not consumed, Because His compassions fail not. They are new every morning; Great is Your faithfulness."

EARLY 1890S AND PREVIOUS EVENTS
CHAPTER 6

"I would have lost heart, unless I had believed; That I would see the
goodness of the Lord; In the land of the living.
Wait on the Lord;
Be of good courage,
And He shall strengthen your heart;
Wait I say, on the Lord!"
Psalm 27: 13-14.

How encouraging these words are! Now it seems best to look at the events of the 1890's in sequence as they unfolded. Moses Hartz Sr. and my Great Great Grandfather, Groffdale John Stoltzfus were married to sisters. The name Groffdale comes from a small town near New Holland near where they lived. John and his first wife, Elizabeth Umble who died in 1853, were the parents of my Great Grandfather John U., and also of Jonas, Great Grandfather of Chris Stoltzfus. John U. was married to Rachel Mast, a twin. Jonas was married to Rachel's sister Catherine. Rachel's twin sister Sarah was married to Benjamin Stoltzfus, first cousin to John U. and Jonas. Benjamin was the bishop during this time at the Conestoga House Amish Church near Morgantown. The twin Rachel named her first child Sarah (my grandmother), and the twin Sarah named her first child Rachel!

Groffdale John's second wife was Elizabeth Nafzinger. She worked for John and his first wife before her death, and stayed on, probably nurturing the children. John and this Elizabeth Nafzinger then were married in 1857, but not until David Mast (presumed to be Moses Hartz's foster father) came to John's house asking for this Elizabeth to be his wife. John went to the house and asked her if she would want this David Mast, or himself. She chose to stay with John. She would have been marrying her sister Magdalena's foster father in law. David's wife Fanny died in 1855, incidently the year that Moses Hartz was ordained. Most of this story is well known. Part of it was learned from "Stoltzfus Nafzinger Family History," by John J. Lapp. He was married to my 1st cousin (which I just learned) and was a Great grandson of Groffdale John and his second wife, and son of Groffdale John and Elizabeth Lapp, close friends of my parents. I imagine that I was in their home as a youngster. I remember when they were overnight guests at our house.

But of all that I have read in recent years about this story, I never have read of the Moses Hartz- David Mast connection in this setting. It is a sign that Moses remains a sore spot in Lancaster County Amish folk-lore, rather not to be mentioned and there is little Nickel Mines kind of "Amish forgiveness" for him, even though he once was officially forgiven and restored, and then the ban was reinstated, And he had not further gone out of bounds.

Moses Hartz was married to Elizabeth's sister Magdalena, thus my great, great, great uncle. The Nafzinger family immigrated from Illbach, Germany with their father Peter and their mother Jacobena. Peter was a minister and had been put in prison for his faith in Christ and is said to have been rather weak by the time the family was made to leave their homeland and sail across the ocean. He (age 37) and one young daughter (Mary, age 4) died and were buried at sea in 1827, during a 10-week voyage.

The parents of Moses immigrated from Germany as Lutherans and left him as an orphan at age four in Berks County, Pa. According to Chris, as he learned from his grandfather, Moses went walking from place to place as a teenager looking for work. He appeared rather energetic when he came to the farm of David Mast, (also my great, great, great uncle) living near Morgantown.

David and his wife Fanny took him in and gave him work on the farm and as a teamster hauling freight by Conestoga wagon to Philadelphia, and west to Pittsburg and beyond. With a German background he fairly well knew the language of his new home and Amish church family where David was a deacon. Moses joined the church and later was married in 1849, raising a family of their own.

In 1855 he was ordained as a minister in the Lower Pequea District, and as mentioned earlier, lived there a few years before locating again in the Conestoga District. He served faithfully a total of forty one years, even after the church divided in 1877. He stayed with the House Amish as the lone minister while other ministers became part of the separated Meeting House Amish, which eventually became known as Conestoga Mennonite Church.

Moses Jr. worked for his brother David near home in the farm related milling industry. When work became scarce in the 1890s due to an economic recession he found work in more distant cities and became an expert in the milling industry. But this kept him away from home much more which was not very pleasing to the Amish church's ideals of family life. He was warned about this, then eventually on April 21, 1895 he was excommunicated and put in the ban to be shunned. His lifestyle was not very pleasing to the Meeting House Amish either so he joined a Mennonite church in the fall of 1895.

His father, a minister but not a bishop, felt that the Scripture reasons for this kind of discipline applied more to pronounced sin, or immorality as some of the applied Scriptures referred to, such as

I Corinthians 5:1 and verse 11. Because he did not hold the meidung against his son, which he was warned that he must do, he was silenced as a minister.

The next spring of 1896, Moses Sr. and his wife joined the Meeting House Church and on July 12, 1896, they also were excommunicated and put in the ban of the House Amish. Their acceptance into the Meeting House Church was surrounded with some controversy as well. They had not made confessions to the House Church and they had been taken in without a bishop officiating. What would all this mean?

1897

CHAPTER 7

"And the Lord passed before him and proclaimed, 'The Lord, the Lord, merciful and gracious, longsuffering, and abounding in goodness and truth. Keeping mercy for thousands, forgiving iniquity and transgression and sin, by no means clearing the guilty, visiting the iniquity of the fathers upon the children and the children's children to the third and fourth generation.'"

-Exodus 34: 6-7.

Ein bedenklich sache. Something to think about. The Almighty is merciful and He is just. He is judge over all the earth, as Abraham said, and makes all things right.

Because of the problems at Conestoga, two bishops, not the same ones as in 1908, were called in from Ohio. They were Christian Stuckey from Fulton County, and Fred Mast from Holmes County, who had roots in the Conestoga Valley. Conestoga had close connections with Millwood where Tennessee John's son Gideon Stoltzfus was bishop. They first had meetings at the Millwood Meetinghouse near Gap, then at the Conestoga church with many members attending.

Chris Stoltzfus talked and wrote about this as told to

him in person by his grandfather Amos J. Stoltzfus son of Jonas. Amos J. witnessed these events as a young man soon to be married. This is also mentioned in Conestoga Church History, by Lamar and Lois Ann Mast.

At the Conestoga meeting on April 16, 1897, Moses and Magdalena were given the choice of going back to the house Amish congregation and starting over, or making confessions right there at the meeting house. Incidentally, their brother in law Groffdale John died only a month earlier on March 22, when there would have been an occasion of many of their relatives and friends to be gathered together at the viewing and at the funeral service and burial. Surely the recent and upcoming events were very much on everyone's minds. To think, that he was an orphan at age 4. Her father and a young sister died on the ocean. At the April 16 meeting, there would have been concern as to what the choices might mean. They decided to make confessions right there. Moses and Magdalena were asked, while on their knees, "Can you confess that you have deserved this sentence that was pronounced upon you?"

His answer was, "Yes, many times have I deserved it." Her answer was, "Yes if this is God's will."

It must have been a most unforgettable experiance for all who were there that day. The two Ohio bishops then reported all this to the house Amish Bishop, Benjamin Stoltzfus, who with his fellow ministers were pleased with the outcome and won approval of the 30 Lancaster County ministers, but as they met with Bishop Ben, one minister named David Beiler Jr. stayed away. The results of that meeting were that peace was restored and the ban was lifted for Moses Sr. and his wife Magdalena. We can believe that there was much rejoicing in Heaven. One could wonder how it is in Heaven now with all those who are gathered together. But because David, a minister but not a bishop disagreed, he later persuaded the other ministers to consent to reinstating the ban, which is what happened. He had the opportunity to speak his peace and forever hold it. But he did not speak up in an orderly way. Peace in the church had been made, but now it was all so abruptly turned upside down. This was a terrible, terrible transgression. An "Ubertreten,"in Deutsch, clearly going out of bounds.

In a similar vein, 115 years later, there are now events unfolding in Ohio involving an Amish bishop, but with a different twist. He and his followers, in what is being called by some to be a cult, have been arrested for going after innocent members of men and women in other Amish communities, clipping off men's beards and cutting off women's hair, all with approval of the bishop. Why? Because he was dissatisfied with the Amish churches because he claimed they were not living right, not strict enough, then he excommunicated several families who had left his community. A committee of a large number of Amish bishops was formed, which decided to overturn that one bishop's decision of wrongly excommunicating families and putting them in the ban. This committee's action which truly was very unusual, was very upsetting to this bishop, so his followers went on the attack. Where is the Golden Rule? Where is the Furcht Gottes? (Fear of God) Where was Brotherly Love?

How could these events in the 1890s in the Conestoga

have happened in a church whose ancestors not long before had escaped similar persecution in their native lands? What did all this mean? Perhaps some answers can be found in the preceding and in the following chapters.

Rooted in the 1890s
Chapter 8

"The Lord is longsuffering and abundant in mercy,
forgiving iniquity and transgression;
but He by no means clears the guilty,
visiting the iniquity of the fathers on the children
to the third and fourth generation."
-Numbers 14:18.

When this is mentioned to relatives or friends, the response is usually to dwell on the first part, while downplaying God's judgements as a just God. Where would we be without His mercy? Or our forefathers in the old country? Nobody is perfect. We all make mistakes, and all have sinned. It is as the Prophet has said, "The Lord has laid on Him the iniquity of us all." Isaiah 53:6. We know that the Lord was merciful to King David in the Bible when he sinned. But still he suffered for his iniquitiy and transgression, and likewise did his descendants bear some of the punishment as God promised King David that they would. Here in Numbers it says that it will be to the third and fourth generation.

After the 1908 meeting when three bishops from Ohio were called to give counsel concerning the "schtreng meidung" which clearly was becoming much more rigid, it was reported that at least one repented. But it does not appear that Minister David Beiler repented of the 1897 transgression or that he tried to make things right. It seems if he would have repented and made a confession, we would know about that just as surely as we know about his transgression. And what about the 30 ministers and bishops whom he persuaded to help with reinstating the ban on the Hartzes, even though they did not further go out of bounds? Two hearts were broken and many more hearts would be broken as time goes on.

What about my own grandfather, who was ordained in 1896, and as a bishop in 1902? It is very likely that he was among the 30 ministers who approved of the transgression. They all should should have made confession in church, and David excommunicated. And my own father, who as a minister and as a bishop, was compelled to uphold the "schtreng meidung," born in 1898 and ordained as a minister in my 1940 birth year, six years after my grandfather passed away. I remember how my father grieved deeply for a fellow minister and bishop in 1955, who because of heavy burdens related to keeping meidung, took his own life. Their mothers were sisters. I would not consider the 30 ministers as having done as badly as Minister David Beiler Jr., but they should have upheld the peace. What about the ageless advice that David could and should have heeded, to "speak now or forever hold your peace?"

It has been said that nobody in Lancaster County ever has had the ban lifted who was no longer in the Old Order Amish Church. That is not true. Those who say that don't know the history or they do not want to accept the truth. It was lifted in this case upon honest confessions on bended knee, and in an orderly way.

My own father, I felt was a loving father of whom I have good childhood memories. Along with my mother they carried a heavy load of raising a family of ten children. He baptized me in 1959, but then officiated in excommunicating me and putting me in the ban to be shunned, 2 ½ years later in 1962. I had my first reality check soon afterward one day when I helped him with barn painting. The peak where I was painting was very high, as barns are in that area. I was using a long 3-section extension ladder, and it was rather scary. He had been at the bottom all the while to steady the ladder and when I came close to the bottom I wanted to quickly lay aside the paint bucket and brush. Without thinking, I handed it to him, as I normally would have, but he refused, telling me to set it on the ground instead. Yes it did become real. He did not accuse me of tempting him to take something from me, and truthfully I did not tempt him. But there have been a number of situations where I was wrongly accused by various people of tempting.

I remember well a summer evening there in 1962 while visiting with him under the maple tree in the front yard where I grew up. He said he felt that the reasons for expelling me were not good enough, not valid, but that the other ministers insisted. The son of one of those ministers, who was later ordained to succeed my father as a minister, told me in recent years in person, before his own death, that he is sorry that as a member the day the church took counsel to excommunicate me, that he consented to it.In 1982 a request was made in writing to lift the ban and given in person by one of our pastors to the bishop who succeeded my Dad.

The reasons for this action were: missing communion twice, and for working for someone who was in the Amish ban. Actually that man was a Mennonite Christian and my day to day work was for his son who had not been Amish. We painted city water towers, even the very tops, suspended by a harness connected to block and tackle, about a hundred feet in the air. At first I did not think I could do it. I did not have a car at this time and I did not join another church (Pequea Amish Mennonite by Bishop Elam Kauffman) until the end of the year. I have always been in the Amish or Mennonite tradition.

It seems that I was told that there was a third reason for expelling me; that I was not present in church when I was summoned. Recently while thinking about this, I was reminded how it was with Jesus when He was on trial. In Mathew 27:12 it is written, "And while He was being accused by the chief priests and elders, He answered nothing." In Isaiah 53:7, the Prophet said, "He was oppressed and He was afflicted, Yet He opened not His mouth; He was led as a lamb to the slaughter. And as a sheep before its shearers is silent, So He opened not His mouth." He did respond in part of His trial, but when charges of wrongdoing were brought against Him, He said nothing, just as the Prophet had foretold. Actually, how could He have answered? He was on trial for our sins and our wrong-doing, for which He could give no defense. Therefore He was sentenced to die. Otherwise the price for our sins would never have been paid and we would all be eternally lost. Oh my.

And so perhaps it was not meant for me to appear in church that day to answer the charges. Because it was as my father had told me that same summer, that the charges against me were not good enough, so it must have been God's will not to answer.

It seems that on that summer night there on the lawn in 1962, that reality hit my father, realizing that because of the tradition of the lifelong "schtreng meidung," that he may never again have a normal father-son relationship with me. It seems he was feeling what many others have felt who went through this, and as it was for Moses Hartz Sr. 62 years earlier, who could not bring himself to shun his own son, who he did not feel was living in sin. Dad probably knew that story well, because of his roots there and also by being in the ministry. We just never had any discussion about it, and I was 42 years younger than he.

That night he expressed a desire for us to meet with my older sister Sarah, (older by five years) who lived several miles west. She and her husband were truly faithful in the Amish faith. He wished we could be together that night yet, and there was some discussion on his part as to how we would get there, to see if this situation could somehow be resolved. It did not work out for us to go. But that night I felt the love of a father for his son, like I perhaps never have felt before or since.

Nevertheless the meidung goes on and on. And nevertheless, I and two older brothers were disinherited in our father's last will and testament of 1968, like deaths in the famly before there were any, (was he pressured to do this?) Could our forefathers , for all they had seen in the old country, have seen this coming? Now, never again to have the rights of a son, which as believers we have with our Heavenly Father, as we read it in the 8th chapter of Romans. Yet I must remember the words there in verse 18: "For I consider that the sufferings of this present time are not worthy to be compared to the glory which shall be revealed in us." I want to be a forgiving person as Christ has forgiven us.

VICTORY IN JESUS
CHAPTER 9

"Therefore purge out the old leaven, that you may be a new lump,
since you truly are unleavened. For indeed Christ,
our Passover, was sacrificed for us."
I Corinthians 5:7.

That is the simple Gospel. Jesus died to save us and to cleanse us, as the children of Israel were saved by the blood that first Passover night in Egypt. Yes, Jesus wants His body, the church to be pure, purged of sin and washed in His blood. Are we washed in the blood?

And then Paul wrote in verse 11 of I Corinthians 5, as I have long remembered it in the King James Version, "Now I have written unto you, not to keep company with any man who is called a brother, be a fornicator, or covetous, or an idolater, or a railer, or a drunkard, or an extortioner; with such a one no not to eat." This verse is about habitual offenders living in sin. It is taught by some to mean the Communion table, by others, common table fellowship around a meal. Why was it written? Because there was a man in the church who "had his father's wife," was presumably living with her in a relationship of incest, which is sin.

But first it says, "not to keep company." As one to whom this Scripture is applied, I have no choice but to take this seriously, and also another often used Scripture in II Thessalonians 3:14 which does not even mention eating, only not keeping company. So how can the meidung mean only not eating, while continuing to keep company with those who are in the ban? Ess kompt net iva ense. It does not agree or make sense, to keep company and to keep the meidung.

I have learned many things the hard way in my experience, to know that I can't pretend that I am not in the ban. I keep saying and writing in cards and letters, that, "If I am no longer in the ban I wish someone would tell me." I desire to live in peace and to be regarded not as an "apostate," but as one who is washed in the blood of our Passover Lamb who died for me. Although I don't believe it, I grew up with the perception that a person under discipline is not victorious, but rather to be pitied.

And now we live in a time of much boldness in sexual immorality, when homosexuality (fornication in many cases and sometimes adultery) is being approved by a president, national and state leaders. That is discrimination, and it is sexism, forsaking and excluding the other gender, and it is what the Bible calls "abomination," which means, not acceptable and it is sin. We recognize that some people struggle with sexual feelings, but approving those feelings to be practiced, is of great concern. Conservatives who become progressives often are double minded and become the most unstable.

Even professing Christians are caught up in this movement, yes even Mennonite Anabaptists, and boasting in it, holding the Word of God in contempt. Nobody is perfect, but we should strive for holiness, and especially leaders in the church, who are called to be "blameless," as Paul wrote to Timothy in I Timothy 3:3. Some are as bold as to say that Jesus did not say anything about it, saying that the judgement that came on Sodom and Gomorrah was about lack of hospitality rather than immorality. (What about Revelation 22:15?) The Scriptures in Genesis and elsewhere show that it clearly was homosexual behavior, sexual immorality. Some churches can't seem to find the courage or the will to use discipline, as it is instructed in the above Scripture by the Apostle Paul. It is grief, wrongly applied or not applied at all. Either way, it is excessive. I believe that's how Paul would have felt. "Oh that my head were waters, And my eyes a fountain of tears, That I might weep day and night for the slain of the daughter of my people." The words of the Prophet Jeremiah in chapter 9:1.

" And many false prophets shall rise, and shall deceive many. And because iniquity shall abound, the love of many shall wax cold. But he that shall endure unto the end, the same shall be saved." Mathew 24:11,12,13. KJV. Will a time come when those who believe in the gay movement so strongly, that they would fight for it as slave owners did, which became the Civil War? Oh how deceitful the heart is.

I am aware that some people from my original homeland

in Pennsylvania come to special treatment facilities for Amish people here in Goshen, Indiana. This is connected to Oaklawn Hospital, and there is a similar place in Pennsylvania called Philhaven Hospital. My fourth and fifth grade teacher, Abe Hostetter, later served there as a doctor.

In early 1969 as a young father and when my wife was close to giving birth to our second child, our only son, before Oaklawn had their present hospital, I was also under its care, for depression. It was hard for me to hold a job. I was admitted to Elkhart General Hospital in a special ward for two weeks, and taken daily to the nearby Oaklawn clinic for therapy. As a young adult this was a very humbling experience, and something I rarely, if ever shared with my birth family in Pa. At least not at that time.

God was good to me, although it was very hard for my family here. He kept us in His loving care and helped us to go on, even as I struggled for many years with occasional depression and the need for counseling several times. The last was in early 2000 with a professional Christian counselor. At that time it became more clear to me that I must acknowledge that I am in the ban, and to accept the Scriptures that the church applies to discipline that come from I Corinthians 5:11 and II Thessalonians 3:14, though wrongly applied. Brother-in-law David in Canada and Sam Bontrager of Woodlawn Church have been very encouraging to me. They are both trained in counseling.

It is very distressing when I am invited to keep company someplace, or even when people invite themselves to our house, and then try to keep the meidung. It is very distressing. While not being in that kind of environment all the time, I sometimes do things that I should not, without thinking, like when I was painting with my Dad, or at a cousins funeral here in Indiana, while at the cafeteria style meal afterward, two unknown couples from Pa. who knew me, who were nearby, got up as soon as I sat down. Then I am accused of tempting. Far be it from me. Is it not rather that I am being tempted, to come and keep company, and then to be shunned? "I cried out to You, O Lord: I said, You are my refuge, my portion in the land of the living." Psalm 142:5.

During my most recent counseling sessions early in the year of 2000, I felt like I was really giving myself up to the discipline and to the Lord, but not submitting myself over and over to keep company, which the Scriptures forbid me to do. I am willing to endure oppression in this way if it is God's will, remembering how Jesus suffered as the righteous for the unrighteous. I marked this occasion in 2000 with a stone, at a special place along a walking path in our woods, where I often spend time in prayer. I placed one stone there every year until there were ten, representing ten in our family. I thought of the time when the children of Israel were delivered by the hand of God as they crossed the swollen Jordan River, in the midst of it on dry ground. One man of each of the twelve tribes was instructed to take a stone from the river bed and to put them on a pile on the other side, which was the Promised Land. It was to be a visual reminder for future generations to see and remember.

DESCENDANTS OF THE 1800'S GENERATION
CHAPTER 10

*"Now faith is the substance of things hoped for,
the evidence of things not seen."*
-Hebrews 11:1.

Once a year, or was it twice, this faith chapter was read in our church service by our deacon.

Minister David Beiler Jr. was married to the oldest of Tennessee John Stoltzfus's fifteen children. John B. Jr., was married to Mary Hartz, daughter of Moses Sr. In 1847, seven month old Salome, daughter of Tennessee John, died and was the first to be buried on the far west corner of John's farm. That later became Millwood Cemetary, where some of my ancestors are buried, including my parents. That is so amazing because it is there that the Millwood Meeting House was built, which along with Conestoga, was a result of the Amish division of 1876-1877 and was followed 20 years later by the "schtreng meidung." So people from both sides of the isle are buried there. This is all so amazing to me.

In the fifteen years since Mother passed away, eight more have passed away, siblings and in-laws. We were all there that day (except 3 who died earlier; Levi, Sarah, and Emanuel, and our parents) as we gathered at sister-in-law Katie's house for a time to be together and for a meal after the burial. They say that time is short. Could they not on this unique occasion have said, why can't we be at one table and eat together as one? Now those eight are no longer with us.

A number of Tennessee John's children did not remain with the house Amish, including son Gideon, a bishop at Millwood and also at Conestoga for a time. Tennessee John, Millcreek John, and Groffdale John were first cousins, all were bishops except apparently the latter, who was a minister.

As mentioned earlier, one of the five bishops at the 1909 occasion who responded to a petition, was Benjamin, son of Minister David Beiler Jr. Benjamin had a son named John who was eleven years younger than my father, and both were ordained as bishop in 1955. I barely knew him but it seems that they were close friends. My parents wanted me to be a friend with one of John's sons who was close to my age, but they lived several miles away. So I really did not know him and that did not happen.

John was asked to have the main sermon at my father's funeral in January of 1977. I remember him well from that occasion, especially regarding a statement he made in his sermon about my father. He said in Pa. Deutsch, "Ich glaub es wa der bruder sei trusht das all sei kinda in der warheit wandela, und ich glaub es sella veg iss." Translated, he said, "I believe it was the brother's desire that all of his children would walk in the truth, and I believe that's the way it is."

I mentioned this to my family, asking Mother, then how can it be that some (three) in the family are still in the ban when he said that's the way it is? She replied, "We hope it is that way." I do not recall exactly, but it seems he may have quoted III John, verse 4 which reads, "I have no greater joy than to hear that my children walk in truth."

Besides Bishop John, I was aquainted with two more of his grandfather David's grandchildren, with good memories. One was Aunt Mary, the second wife of my Uncle Jonathan, Dad's brother. She was always kind to me, at their house and at ours. Also Aaron Glick, a long time and highly respected minister at Weavertown and Pequea churches. Aaron gave a message at our 1964 wedding, with I Peter 3:1-7 as the text. I did not know of his family tree at that time, or of Aunt Mary's family, or of John's.

"Wait on the Lord; Be of good courage; And He shall strengthen your heart; Wait I say on the Lord." Psalm 27:14. I often think of these words. They are a comfort and strength to many who believe and trust in Him.

Through the years as I have pondered over the words of Bishop John Beiler, it seemed to me that as he affirmed my father in this way that it was sort of a confession of wrongdoing on the part of his grandfather, and to an extent, also on the part of their two bishop fathers. But I have to realize that it may only be wishful thinking on my part. The real confession for the transgression (ubertretton) in 1897 has never been made right that I know of. Is it too late?

Whatever, the lifelong "schtreng meidung" as it took hold in 1897, goes on and on. Meanwhile many of the Amish freely use their own cell phones, and line telephones in designated places, while some work away from home at distant places. Some modern conveniences that were once not acceptable but are now, are in use and making Moses Hartz Jr. who was excommunicated for these things, look like child's play. Where is the forgiveness for the once unacceptable practices? "No weapon forged against you will prevail, and you will refute every tongue that accuses you. This is the heritage of the servants of the Lord, and this is their vindication from me, declares the Lord" Isaiah 54:17. NIV

1809-1766

CHAPTER 11

"For the death that He died, He died to sin once for all;
but the life He lives, He lives to God.
Likewise you also, reckon yourselves to be dead indeed to sin,
but alive to God in Jesus Christ our Lord."
-Romans 6:11.

This is my testimony, to be dead to sin, not dead in sin. 1809 is the birth year of two notable men, on the same day in fact. First, Abraham Lincoln, who as president helped to free many people from the bondage of slavery. And Charles Darwin, who as an evolutionist has led many people astray from the Biblical account of creation, which reads, "In the beginning God created the heavens and the Earth." Genesis 1:1.

What about the reference to a ministers conference in 1809 that was mentioned here in Chapter 4, as was referred to in the bishops response in 1909? I wondered quite a while about that after I read the response to the 35 families. What did they mean by the writings of Bishop David Beiler of 1861?

I have not seen his actual writings, if indeed they still exist.

I finally found the answer in Lamar Mast's, "As Long As Wood Grows and Water Flows," pages 32-33. As is sometimes the case, there seems to have been a lack of spirituality in the church. The Methodists were meeting some of that need with evangelistic meetings and with the presence of a number of Methodist churches in the Morgantown area which drew away some of the Amish people, where the leaders understandably became alarmed. According to the Mast writings a "group of the ministers from the upper district, thought to be the congregations of Mifflin and Somerset Counties, and the lower district, thought to encompass all congregations in Berks, Lancaster, and Chester Counties, met at a home, probably in the Lancaster-Berks area, where the largest congregation of Amish Mennonites lived at the time. The nine articles which follow were drawn up at that time."

PENNSYLVANIA - OCTOBER 17,1809

"Articles of agreement, discussed and decided by the ministers of the upper and lower districts.

First: That all those of our members who leave us to join other churches shall be treated as apostate persons according to the word of the Lord and his ordinance, and shall be separated and shall be recognized as subjects for the ban.

Second: Permission shall be given to "admonish" at a funeral in our brotherhood, but not outside.

Third: We have no basis in scripture for excluding any member from taking part in the council of the church.

Fourth: That shunning shall be exercised toward banned persons according to the teaching of Christ and the apostles with respect to eating and drinking, life and work ("Handel and Wandel") until they are again received by the church.

Fifth : Anyone who transgresses the rule of shuning in weakness or ignorance can be reconciled by confession to the church that he has erred; whoever transgresses intentionally but is not stubborn about it when admonished, can be reconciled by a "full' (hoechst") confession, but whoever stubbornly refuses to hearken to admonition shall be excommunicated from the church.

Sixth: Whoever swears an oath knowingly and frivolously shall be excommunicated; but whoever swears out of inexperience shall be required to make "full" confession.

Seventh: In regard to cutting off the hair and beard, it is decided that no one shall be accepted as a member in the church unless he manifests the full fruit of obedience, and all those who are already in the church and are not willing to be obedient to the regulation shall be dealt with according to Christian discipline ("Ordnung").

Eighth: It is decided that jury service shall not be tolerated or permitted for brethren in the church.

Ninth : Proud dresses, proud trousers, hats, and combs in the hair, and similar worldly clothing shall not be tolerated in the church.

In conclusion: All the above articles shall be observed and practiced according to Christian discipline and patience."

Acknowledged and signed by us.

Michael Lapp	Hannes Lapp
Johannes Blanck	Peter Blanck
David Yoder	Christian Miller
Christel Stoltzfus	Christian Stutzman
Johannes Konig	Jacob Miller
Christian Yoder	Daniel Zug
Christian Hertzler	Christian Zug
Hannes Yoder	Isaac Yoder
Hannes Beiler	Jacob Stutzman
Christian Konig	Daniel Miller
Christian Zug	Abraham Muller
Joseph Kurtz	

Mast adds this footnote: "At the time of the Conference, all of the involved ministers agreed with the new resolution, but as time passed, many of them regretted their actions, causing disunity once again." This resolution does somewhat follow the 1632 Dordrecht Confession of Faith, but lacking the various Scripture references, which references seem to give the 1632 document better grounding. Doctrines and confessions truly need to be rooted in the Word of God. The Dordrecht Confession, which I understand is still followed by the Old Order Amish, does that quite well, in each of the eighteen articles.

Regarding the first article; the word "apostate" as used here seems rather strong. Let us hold more closely to the teachings of the Apostle Paul in I Corinthians chapter 5, where he says in verse 7, "Therefore purge out the old leaven, that you may be a new lump, since you truly are unleavened. For indeed Christ, our Passover, was sacrificed for us," And one wonders if "apostates" is what our forefathers were called in their native countries who joined Anabaptist churches and were persecuted. Is it pleasing to God to call someone an apostate who has made an honest confession and has proven by their testimony and fruit bearing, to have been washed in the Blood of Christ?

Also, it seems that the words in the fourth article "until they are again received by the church," has been wrongly interpreted by some to mean only one particular church, only the church from where they were expelled. We must recognize that organizations have the prerogative or right to establish and maintain memberships in their organizations and to keep order, but with expectations to be reasonable. The "Schtreng Meidung" (strict shunning) which was begun after the transgression against Moses and Magdalena Hartz later, in 1897, where a person can be forgiven only by coming back to the same bishop or church district, or a district in the area, does not appear to be grounded in the above nine articles, certainly not in the Dordrecht Confession, not in the teachings of Christ and the apostles.

The one signature, "Christel Stoltzfus," we would presume to be Christian, son of immigrant Nicholas. They arrived at Philadelphia October 18, 1766, when the young son was 17. He was ordained in 1800 as a bishop. Did he forget so quickly how it was in their native country for his parents and for many others of the faith who were cut off and persecuted? What has been gained?

One could wonder if immigrant Jacob Mast, who was ordained as a bishop in 1788 and died in 1808, one year before this, would have signed on to the nine articles. It seems that to write this resolution right after his death was a rather poor reflection on Jacob's many years of faithfulness to the Lord and to his calling. He clearly had a heart of a shepherd who cared for his sheep, whether they be lost or found. Of course releasing those who find other pastures can be painful. But that's what they did in the 1876-1877 divisions at Millwood and at Conestoga, and when 35 families left because of the "schtreng meidung" in 1909 while trying to do something about it, and in the county wide division of 1966. For some of us there is no end in sight, except Heaven. When our forefathers in the old country were not released, they were persecuted instead, some even to the point of death. "And behold I am coming quickly, and My reward is with Me, to give to every one according to his work." Revelation 21: 12.

EPILOGUE

"He who testifies to these things says, 'Surely I am coming quickly.'
Amen. Even so, come, Lord Jesus!"
- Revelation 22:20.

Let us now devote this last part to the Mast family. C.Z. Mast and Robert E. Simpson were the authors of the 1942 highly regarded book; "Annals of Conestoga Valley." C.Z. Mast, a six generation descendant of immigrant Jacob Mast, and my father's second cousin, also compiled "Mast Family History," published in 1911. Here on page 67 he writes, "Mr. (David) Mast as an Amish Mennonite Deacon was presumably successor to his father (John) in the congregation of Conestoga Valley, which was founded about 1765 by his grandfather, Bishop Jacob Mast, and afterwards became the first permanent Amish Mennonite settlement in America." This was one year before Nicholas Stoltzfus arrived in Philadelphia. I am a seven generation descendant of both. What follows now is by Christian (C.Z.) Mast in Mast Family History, pages 17-22. Permission from Masthof Press is much appreciated.

"LIFE SKETCH OF BISHOP JACOB MAST."

Bishop Jacob Mast was born in 1738 in Switzerland of Swiss parents. He immigrated to America an orphan boy in company with his four sisters and younger brother John, all were in care of their uncle Johannes Mast, whom we have no record of his remaining days in this country. By tradition he was an aged widower or bachelor, and was presumably buried on the farm now owned by Mr. George D. Fahrenbach of Penn Twp., Berks Co., Pa. The old cemetery is in a dilapidated condition, by which a new barn has been erected, almost covering the whole burial plot.

The party had sailed from Rotterdam in the ship Brotherhood, John Thompson, Captain, landing in Philadelphia, Pa. on Nov. 3, 1750. They selected their home near the site of the Blue Mountains, tradition says. All other early Amish Mennonites formed their first settlement in America at this place, which was known for nearly a century as the "Northkill Congregation." The early members had located in Heidelberg, Lower Heidelberg, North Heidelberg, Penn, Bern, Upper Bern, Center, Upper Tulpehocken, and Jefferson townships, Berks Co. Pa. The majority had lived in the vicinity of the Schuylkill River between Irish Creek and Northkill, where they had opened out farms. From 1754 to 1764 and even at a later period the settlement was exposed and almost exterminated by the torch, hatchet and scalping knife of the savages, and their midnight assault and slaughter. Hundreds fell victims to the relentlessly cruel savages, along the Blue mountains south and north of it, and along the Susquehanna, as far north as Penn's Creek. Among the massacred were many Germans—more than three hundred in all, including such as Hochstetler, Miller, Hartman and Schleich which are family names popularly known in this history. Bishop Jacob Mast and his new life companion and father-in-law, Michael Holly, who had immigrated to America on the same vessel with the remaining members of the Mast family. had now resided nearly ten years in the district of the Northkill congregation of Amish Mennonites. While thus in 1760 they were attacked by Indians and forced to seek another asylum from persecution by settling in Conestoga Valley, on a fertile tract of land forming the watershed between the Schuylkill River and the few larger tributaries of the beautiful Conestoga Creek, which name bears the signification of an Indian tribe, while on its banks are still found numerous Indian relics, such as darts and tomahawks.

A warrant was granted to Bishop Jacob Mast and a certain John Holly, Nov. 19, 1764, and the latter on Apr. 13, 1769 lawfully discharged all the rights and half part of the land to the former. The tract contained 170 acres and an allowance of six per cent for roads which was situated partly in the counties of Berks and Chester. It was purchased from Samuel Martin of Tredyfrin township, Chester Co., Pa., for 325 pounds. On this tract of land Bishop Jacob Mast erected a comfortable log farm house, close to a lusty spring which flows directly from a stratum of limeless sandstone.

His Brother John wandered through the wilderness to Randolph Co., N.C., which the reader may notice a brief account of his lineal descendants contained in the latter part of this volume and also a sketch of his sister Magdalena. The other three sisters are supposed to have died unmarried and buried near the spot of our progenitor, representing graves without inscriptions.

Here the once and again persecuted and oppressed Swiss family, separated from friends and much that makes life agreeable, hoped to unmolestedly begin the world anew. Here, surrounded on all sides by several clans of Indians they located in the gloomy, silent shades of a virgin forest, whose undisturbed solitude was yet uncheered by the murmurs of the honey bee, or the twitterings of the swallow, those neverfailing attendants upon the woodman's ax. For the hum and the warblings of those, they had not only the shout and song of the tawny sons of the forest, but also the nocturnal howlings of the ever watchful dog, baying at the sheeny queen of the night as she moved stately on, reflecting her borrowed light. By way of variety, we imagine their ears were nightly greeted by the shrill, startling whoop of the owl or the crickets wail in the contiguous thickets.

Presumably the Mast family were the first Amish Mennonite settlers to establish and organize a congregation of its kind in Conestoga valley which was the third settlement and the first permanent one in America. It is still known as the "Conestoga congregation."

Bishop Jacob Mast was elected to his office in 1788, was well educated for the times, and was a man of extensive influence. He always visited the various congregations on horseback, riding through dense forests, over great mountains and fording swelling streams, in which his life was also endangered by the red man of the forest. Yet he was in every way adapted to this situation. His preparation was of the best order; and being undoubtedly driven from his native land by religious persecution, he must have rejoiced in finding such a pleasant situation, such inviting conditions. He knew the suffering of his forefathers through the days of martyrdom , his uncertain condition in his native land, and thus a sense of well-being induced his uncle Johannes to leave with him and his brother and four sisters. But in leaving the valleys and the beautiful mountain scenery of Switzerland so dear to him, he came to possess and enjoy a country equally favored for beauty, for health and for profit; and it was more highly favored in respect to a condition which was to him more important than all others combined__freedom.

He was sound, hopeful and trustful in religious conviction, which had fitted him admirably for his vocation.

He made many visits to his congregations, at least semiannually, of which there were three located in Somerset and Cambria counties, Pennsylvania, known as Gladyes," "Conemaugh" and Castleman's River," two in Chester County, Pennsylvania, (called Chester Valley and Compassville), two in Lancaster County, Pennsylvania (called Conestoga and Pequea), and three in Berks Co,. Pennsylvania__ one in Cumru, one in Maiden Creek and the third in Bern Township (called Northkill).

The Mast family in America have sprung from an ancestry whose lines are well marked as far as they can be traced. These lines however are mainly found within the limits of agricultural industry, genuine morality and sincere earnestness in the performance of the duties of the Christian religion, coupled with a sincere faith in its saving power. There are only several incidents where fame of arms-bearing or military skill was ever attached to any bearing the name of Mast.

The records of American history are practically silent and have little knowledge of the name. But the records of the Christian Church, especially of that branch of it known as the Amish Mennonite Church, are alive with names of pioneers and heroes in the several generations of Masts that have lived since the establishment of the Church in America. First and foremost among these stands the name Jacob Mast, whom fancy pictures as a tall man, having a large and well-proportioned frame, very muscular, with light hair and blue eyes, a face indicating great firmness and resolution, and a body capable of enduring great hardships. How nearly this fancied representation of him may correspond with truth, cannot be said. But of this there is proof, that he was of great mental and moral force, practiced simplicity in attire, being a faithful and zealous servant for his Master and did much to advance the interests of his church.

In the year 1808 he gave up the wonderfully busy life when in the same year his neighbors carried his body out of his old home and buried it in a quiet spot on the broad acres he had tended and loved. His grave is marked with a carved sandstone bearing inscription near the northwest corner of the wall of what is known as Pine Grove Cemetery. His wife, Magdalene

Holly, died Oct. 26, 1820, aged 80 years, and is buried by his side.

Their children had strong constitutions and in general had good health and lead temperate, moral, honest Christian lives and imparted these same good qualities to their children and grandchildren, for which give God the glory. During their childhood days they were commanded before retiring at night to all repeat our Lord's Prayer in concert.

P.S. Writing this postscript may seem out of order. But I remember this day as being exactly ten years, when an older brother passed away on April 23, 2003. He died suddenly of a heart attack as he and his wife were driving down the road in their horse drawn carriage, about a mile from their home. As a young boy, I quite often was his handy man on his farm, with good memories.

Much of what I have written became new to me this last third of my life, certainly since my father passed away in 1977. Even with my mother, who passed away in 1998 and had a clear and sharp mind to her final years, there was little discussion on these things But on one occasion about 20 years ago, while visiting with her at home, in an isolated comment, she said, "My grandmother weighed 300 pounds." At that time I had little interest in extended family, so I did not ask more about that. It was not untill some time later while reading "Golden Memories of Amos J. Stoltzfus" by Chris Stoltzfus about his grandfather, that I learned who this grandmother was. She was Sarah, daughter of the aforementioned Minister

Daniel Mast. She once became impatient with her husband
David F., in his delay in coming for dinner, and took matters
into her own hands. I wish I could say what she did.

On the day of Mother's funeral I took my present family
to another cemetery (Planks # 17) where many of Mother's
extended family is buried. In what seemed like a landmark, a
cedar was growing between the graves of these grandparents,
resting in peace. Peter Nafsinger was buried in the ocean while
immigrating and according to Revelation 20:13, the sea will
give up the dead at the resurrection of the dead when Jesus
comes again. Peter's wife Jacobena was the mother in law of
Groffdale John Stoltzfus, by his second marriage, and of Moses Hartz Sr. For some time I have been aware, according
to "Fisher Family History" that beginning with Jacobena and
daughter Elizabeth, John's second wife, a variant name , Bena,
then a daughter Elizabeth, has been alternating like this for
at least seven generations. One of my cousins, no longer living, was married to one of these Benas. She was a daughter of
another Groffdale John, (Lapp), and his wife Elizabeth, who
were close friends of my parents. The name Lena, a variant of
Magdalena, Moses' wife, is very common.

Mother was the best cook. But although we could breathe
the same air, yet we could not eat at the same table, though not
living in sin. Whenever I wrote to her (monthly) I prayed that
it would be acceptable for the mail carrier to deliver the cards
and letters to her, knowing she could not receive them from
my hand. She wrote just as often. She once gave me a letter
to give to another family member, where we were going for a

visit. When we arrived there, without thinking, I handed the letter over but was told to lay it on the table instead. Was it wrong for me to keep company, while they were keeping mei-dung? I know she enjoyed gardening, but I'm afraid she paid a price with pain by working on her knees on the wet ground so much. I stopped working that way a long time ago when I started getting similar knee problems, and instead used a sitting bucket and sometimes simply harvested by stooping.

Exactly one month ago today, March 23,2013, I was involved in a near fatal head on collision in my pickup truck about a mile from our home in mid afternoon. As I saw the car rushing toward me from the other side of the road, I did not expect to survive. But the angel of the Lord brought me through, with only a left shoulder injury, needing a month of therapy, a result of accidently breaking the glass in the door, while the air bag and seat belt were also factors. The police said that, based on their years of experience in working with collisions like this, that I should not be alive. But here I am, by the mercies of God. It must not have been my time, even though I am ready to meet my Maker. Should'nt we all be ready?

I think of a letter which I wrote (I have a copy) to a brother on March 23,2003, exactly ten years before this accident. It was written just after a Sunday after noon nap and a dream (also in my diary). I was outside the barn in Pennsylvania at the site where a horse with a sore shoulder caused a severe head injury for me, on June 23, 1955. In the dream, I was being helped into an ambulance, while my oldest brothers and their wives were coming toward our place a quarter mile away from the South. The wives were shouting in Deutsch, "Yonie, geh net aveck, waht mohl." "don't go away, wait." When they arrived the four oldest brothers came into the ambulance, and then the dream ended. The ambulance was closed, with a rear door, just as the one that took me to the hospital this Spring. I did not go away, or die (in the dream) except to go to the hospital, a couple days after the 1955 accident. Nor did I go away in death this Spring, except to go to the hospital because of a shoulder injury. I was seated behind the cab, next to the car driver who was on a stretcher, both facing the back door. On the way, the paramedic asked her, "Is it true that at 8 oclock this morning, you were at this hospital for medical treatment for a pancreatitis attack (pancreas) and you were told not to be driving?" She said "yes".

I had written this story while we were camping on the shores of Lake Superior in northern Michigan last fall of 2012, and typed it during the winter, yet not knowing just what God has planned for it.

I will close with the words of Romans 12:1and 2, "I beseech you therefore, brethren, by the mercies of God, that you present your bodies a living sacrifice, holy, acceptable to God, which is your reasonable service.

And do not be conformed to this world, but be transformed by the renewing of your mind, that you may prove what is that good and acceptable and perfect will of God."

The homeplace near Cains in 1973.

The author's son Curtis and father, 1973.

Buena Vista School 1907

Teacher Anna Hershey. 1st row Paul Stoltzfus, Aaron Stoltzfus, unknown, Earl Rhoads, Katie Stoltzfus, Florence Howe, Emma Stoltzfus, Barbara Lapp, Lizzie Lapp, Lizzie Stoltzfus, Betsy Stoltzfus, unknown, Ada Spence. 2nd row Elmer Stoltzfus, John K. Lapp, Levi Stoltzfus, Chester Rhoad, John Hoover, John Spence, Lizzie Spence, Susie Stoltzfus, Fannie Stoltzfus, Naomi Stoltzfus, Fannie Stoltzfus, Edna Rhoads, Joann Hoover, Bertha Evans, Ruth Stoltzfus, Sara Lapp John Reeser, Sam Stoltzfus.

Included here are the author's mother, Katie Stoltzfus and siblings Betsy, Levi and Sam. (Courtesy, brother Gid)

They met at their Waterloo in 1938

This photo includes four of the author's brothers; David, Aaron, Levi and Gideon. Front Row: Amos Blank, Lewis Hillard, Christ Stauffer, Robert Refford, Ralph Samuels, William Cauller, Levi Stoltzfus, Gideon Stoltzfus. Second Row: William Englerth, Bob Baldwin, Anna Stauffer, Louise Wanner, Fanny Blank, Shirley Jackson, June Kruger, Alfred Baldwin, Mary Stauffer, Esther Ann Hershey, Verna Stauffer. Third Row: Dolly Pratt, Benjamin Yoder, Miriam Kauffman, Paul Plank, Aaron Stoltzfus, Walter Plank. Fourth Row: Guy Wanner, Gerald Hershey, James Miller, Miss Connell, Teacher, David Stoltzfus, Ruth Plank. (Credit, Louise Wanner Wenger)

Waterloo Apartment, 1946. This photo was taken when the author (in front looking left) was perhaps not yet enrolled at Waterloo School, a couple hundred feet from the South end of Churchtown Road at Cains. The teacher, Ruth Guy, is in back under the door bracket, with an older brother Emanuel next, behind sister Sarah, then a brother Sammie, all along the crack in photo, taken in about 1946. Many of the other names are forgotten. The Bible teachers in front are Mr. and Mrs. Harry Brubaker, with students holding up their Gideons New Testaments. (Courtesy, sister Sarah)

Marchand's celery fields in 1954

The author's present home place, N. 23rd St. Goshen, IN.
(Courtesy, Goshen Historical Society.)

The author's children; Lonna, Curtis and Rosetta, held by wife Mar-
ietta, on what became known as Rosie's sledding hill in East Goshen.

Our source of water power on the Pequea Creek.

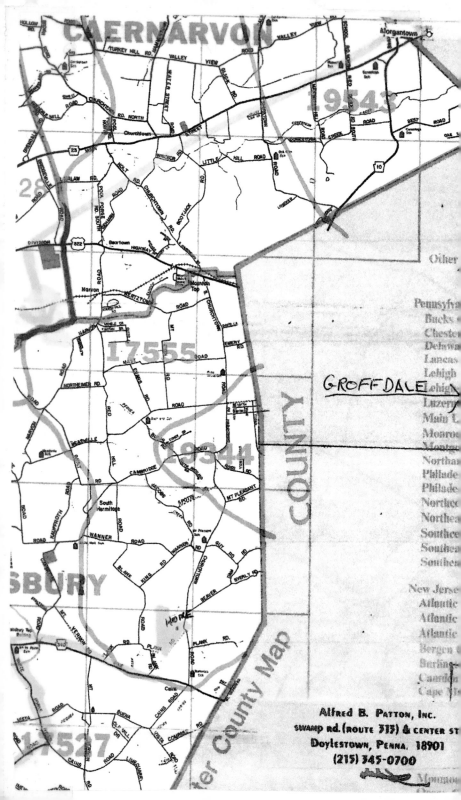